NATURE'S FURY

TSUNAMI!

Anne Rooney

FRANKLIN WATTS
LONDON • SYDNEY

First published in 2006 by
Franklin Watts
338 Euston Road
London NW1 3BH

Franklin Watts Australia
Hachette Children's Books
Level 17/207 Kent St, Sydney, NSW 2000

Produced by Arcturus Publishing Limited,
26/27 Bickels Yard, 151–153 Bermondsey Street, London SE1 3HA

Editor: Alex Woolf
Design: www.mindseyedesign.co.uk
Picture researcher: Glass Onion Pictures

Picture credits
Corbis: 4, 7, 16 (Punit Paranjpe/Reuters), 18 (Kim Kyung-Hoon/Reuters),
22 (Lloyd Cluff), 23 (Sukree Sukplang/Reuters), 24 (Babu/Reuters),
26 (Wolfgang Kaehler), 27 (Bazuki Muhammad/Reuters).

Rex Features: 10 (Sipa Press), 14 (Sipa Press), 15 (Sipa Press),
17, 19, 20 (SS/Keystone USA), 21, 29 (Twentieth Century Fox/Everett).

Science Photo Library: 5 (Chris Butler), 6 (US Geological Survey),
8 (Gary Hincks), 9, 11 (David Hardy), 12 (Sally Bensusen),
13 (Carlos Munoz-Yague/LDG/Eurelios), 28 (John Foster).

Zul Mukhida: 25.

Every attempt has been made to clear copyright. Should there be any
inadvertent omission, please apply to the publisher for rectification.

Anne Rooney asserts her moral right to be recognized as the author of this work.

A CIP catalogue record for this book is available from the British Library

Dewey Decimal Classification Number: 554.46'37

ISBN 07496 6613 7

Printed in China

Contents

What is a Tsunami?

A tsunami is a huge wave that can flood the land with devastating effects. The word *tsunami* is Japanese for 'harbour wave'. It is an appropriate name, as it is when a tsunami hits a harbour or other area used by people that its destructive power is felt. It can flood towns and villages with little warning, destroying all in its path and killing people and animals. When the wave retreats, everything can be swept out to sea.

Tsunamis through time

There have probably been tsunamis for as long as there has been sea. One of the earliest descriptions was left by the Greek historian Thucydides, who described a tsunami in the Mediterranean Sea near Greece in 426 BCE: 'The sea … returned in a huge wave and invaded a great part of the town, and retreated leaving some of it still under water; so that what was once land is now sea; such of the

▼ *A tsunami floods houses in Oahu, Hawaii, in 1957.*

inhabitants perishing as could not run up to the higher ground in time.' Thucydides linked the tsunami to recent earthquakes in the area – modern scientists would do the same.

What causes tsunamis?

Tsunamis are caused by a disturbance in or under the sea that makes a large volume of water move suddenly. Most are caused by earthquakes – though landslides, volcanic eruptions and even meteorites falling into the sea can cause tsunamis. Waves flow outwards in a circle from the point where the disturbance happens – like ripples spreading from a stone dropped in a pond.

▲ *A tsunami can have devastating effects if it strikes an area where people live and work.*

CASE STUDY

When the sea and sky fell

Modern geologists point to evidence of a tsunami caused by a meteorite striking the Tasman Sea between 500 and 850 years ago. This may explain a legend told by the people of Burragorang in New South Wales, Australia. One steamy, hot night the people lay unable to sleep in their camp. Just after sunset, the sky shuddered, heaved and tumbled, crashing down on them. The Milky Way split and stars fell – including a gigantic, burning blue star that tore the ground apart, showering the people with chunks of earth and rock. Later, other tribes told of the whole ocean falling on them from above. It then rained for weeks and the whole land was flooded. The native peoples believed these events were caused by an angry ancestor in the sky.

The Tsunami Zone

Tsunamis can happen anywhere, but most occur around the Pacific Ocean. Volcanic eruptions and earthquakes are very common around the edges of the Pacific, both inland and just off the coast, and these can trigger tsunamis that spread across the whole ocean.

Inland tsunamis

Tsunamis can even happen in an inland sea or lake. There have been many tsunamis in the Mediterranean Sea, which is largely enclosed by Europe and North Africa. Earthquakes and volcanic activity around Italy and Greece have caused some disastrous tsunamis through history, including some believed to have destroyed ancient Greek and Minoan cities thousands of years ago. Smaller bodies of water, like lakes and rivers, can also be affected by tsunamis. In 1811, New Madrid in the USA was struck by the largest earthquake in recorded American history and the flow of the Mississippi River was reversed. The eruption of Mount Saint Helens in Washington State in 1980 caused a tsunami on nearby Spirit Lake.

▲ *The Ring of Fire is a zone prone to earthquakes and volcanic eruptions that circles the Pacific Ocean.*

Landfall

A tsunami can strike land a long way from the event that causes it – even on the other side of the ocean. In 1946, a tsunami that struck the Hawaiian Islands in the middle of the Pacific Ocean was caused by an earthquake in the Aleutian Trench, off the coast of Alaska, five hours earlier. The earthquake was over four thousand kilometres from Hawaii.

When a tsunami strikes a region that did not feel the earthquake, it can seem to come from nowhere. When it reaches the shore quickly and near to the source of the earthquake or eruption, it brings new devastation to an area hit only minutes before.

EARTH'S JIGSAW

The surface, or crust, of the Earth is divided into chunks called tectonic plates that fit together in a giant jigsaw. There are seven large plates and several smaller ones. The Pacific Ocean is held on a single vast plate.

Within the Earth, semi-liquid, red-hot rock moves very slowly around the globe, dragging the plates with it. At the joins between plates, they rub or push against each other. These are geologically active areas where earthquakes and volcanic eruptions happen.

▼ *A lone man watches the approach of the tsunami that swept him away on Hilo's Pier 1 in Hawaii in 1946.*

Earthquakes and Tsunamis

The Earth's tectonic plates move slowly – about the same speed as your fingernails grow. But where they push or grind together, pressure can build up over years or centuries. When the tension becomes too great, the plates slip with a jolt, causing an earthquake.

Earthquake area

At the edges of the ocean, the ocean plate pushes against the plates carrying land. As it is denser than the continental plates, the oceanic plate is forced downwards at pressure. It melts, and some of it goes down to be reabsorbed into the Earth's mantle, but some rises to feed volcanoes. Sometimes a piece of plate may be snapped off or flicked upwards, making an earthquake. More than eighty percent of the tsunamis in the Pacific over the last two thousand years have been caused by earthquakes.

▶ *At the edges of the ocean, the Earth's crust carrying the sea is pushed down below the edge of the continent. Earthquakes and volcanic eruptions are common in these areas.*

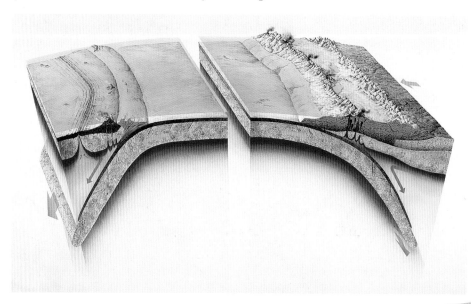

Filling the gap

When the Earth's crust under the sea suddenly slips, a massive column of water may fall quickly downwards, rushing in to fill a gap, or it may be rapidly thrust upwards. Under gravity, the water immediately evens out, correcting itself to regain a smooth surface. As it does so, a series of massive waves is thrown out.

If there is an earthquake on land but near the coast, ripples of energy, just like waves on water but moving more slowly, run through the solid ground. When they meet the sea, the waves are transferred to waves in the water. Some quite small earthquakes on land translate into gigantic and dangerous tsunamis.

◀ *Immediately after a terrible earthquake shook the Portuguese city of Lisbon in 1755, a giant tsunami devastated the area.*

CASE STUDY

Lisbon, 1755

On 1 November 1755, Lisbon in Portugal was rocked by one of the most powerful earthquakes in recorded history. Lasting ten minutes, it measured 9.0 on the Richter scale (a scale for measuring earthquake intensity) and demolished much of the city. People fled to the beach to escape falling buildings, but when a huge tsunami struck minutes later, many were killed. The tsunami also affected other parts of Europe and even reached North Africa and the Caribbean. A third of the population of Lisbon died, and over 100,000 people in total. Modern earthquake research began with this disaster.

Volcanoes and Tsunamis

The very same areas that are plagued by earthquakes also suffer volcanic eruptions. As the oceanic crust is forced downwards, it melts underground. Some rises through the Earth's upper layer to swell vast magma chambers beneath volcanoes. When a volcano can hold no more, the magma is hurled out under pressure, making an eruption.

Scalding molten rock explodes into the air, sometimes blowing away part of the volcano itself. When the magma chamber has emptied, the weight of the mountain above often comes crashing down into the empty space, causing the volcano to collapse inwards.

▼ *A volcanic eruption in Soufrière Hills, Montserrat, in 1997. Eruptions in this area have often started tsunamis.*

Water and fire

If a volcano is on the coast, or is an island in the sea, water and molten rock make an explosive mixture. Water rushing into the magma chamber often causes an explosion so violent the volcano is blown apart, and the sudden movement of a large volume of water can cause a tsunami. A tsunami may also happen if huge chunks of rock are thrown into the sea by an eruption. Many volcanoes are completely underwater. An undersea eruption can force a column of water upwards, or the sea floor can collapse into an emptying magma chamber. Either event can cause a tsunami.

Combined assault

Earth tremors – minor earthquakes – can be the first sign that a volcano is about to erupt. Either the earth tremors or the eruption itself can cause a tsunami, and often an area will be devastated by more than one disaster in a short period of time.

▲ *The Greek island of Thera (Santorini) as it may have looked before 1410 BCE when its volcano exploded, and as it looks now.*

CASE STUDY

Krakatau, 1883

The Indonesian island of Krakatau blew apart in a massive volcanic eruption in August 1883. After months of activity, a fissure opened up in the volcano and seawater poured in. When the water met hot molten rock, the whole island exploded. As the sea rushed into the gaping hole where the island had been, a huge tsunami swept the area, larger than any seen before. About 36,000 people died around the coasts of surrounding lands. Boats were carried far in shore and buildings were swept out to sea. Rafts of volcanic rock, ripped up trees, debris and dead bodies floated for months, travelling as far as the coast of Africa.

Watery Build-up

A tsunami may start far out at sea or near the coast. In the area of the Ring of Fire, there are often volcanic eruptions and earthquakes near the coast. An earthquake under the water makes a series of waves that travel outwards in a circle from the epicentre (starting point) of the quake, like ripples from a stone dropped in a pond, or like the waves pushed out of the way by a surfacing submarine.

On the side nearest the shore, the waves reach land quickly – often before there has been time to warn people living in the area. The wave that strikes the coast nearby is called a local tsunami. But waves travel outwards in all directions and some cross the ocean to hit land many hundreds or even thousands of kilometres away – a distant tsunami.

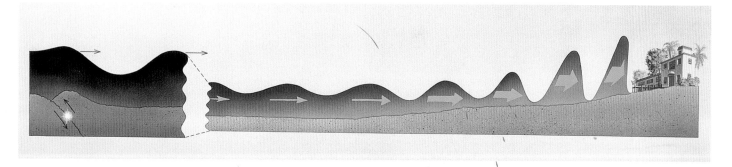

▲ *When it is far out to sea the tsunami is small but moves quickly. As it approaches shore, it slows down and grows much taller.*

Starting small

Far out at sea, the tsunami is a tiny wave, but can travel as fast as a commercial jet – over 750 kilometres per hour. The height of the wave may be only sixty centimetres, and so it often goes unnoticed by ships in the area.

As the tsunami approaches land and the water gets shallower, the wave slows down and grows much taller. By the time it reaches the shore, it can be thirty metres tall, or even taller, and slow to fifty kilometres per hour. There can be as much as a thousand tonnes of water hitting each metre of coastline.

Spot a tsunami

	Normal wave	Tsunami
Speed	8–100 km per hour	800–1,000 km per hour
Wave period (time between two waves)	5–20 seconds	10 minutes to 2 hours
Wave length (distance between two waves)	100–200 m	100–500 km

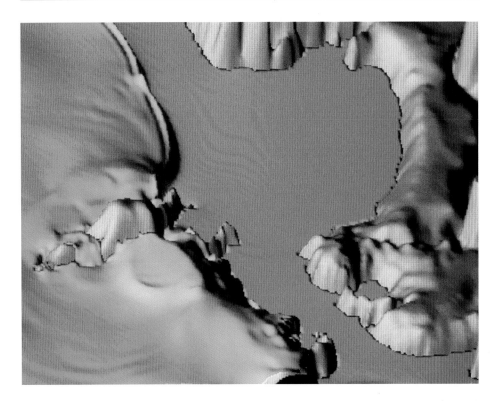

◀ *A computer model of the tsunami caused by the Lisbon earthquake in 1755, about an hour after the quake.*

WHY DOES A TSUNAMI GROW SO TALL?

The energy of the wave remains much the same, just dropping slightly as it travels, because of friction with the sea-bed. When it is out at sea, the energy is dispersed through the whole depth of the wave, but as the water becomes shallower near the coast the water is forced upwards by the compressed energy.

Minute by Minute

A tsunami can bring total devastation in just a few terrifying minutes. The most destructive tsunamis are those that strike without warning, as it takes most people only about ten minutes to move to safety if they know a tsunami is on its way.

In some cases, the sea draws back before the tsunami strikes, and sometimes before it is even visible. This is the wave pulling the sea into itself. On the shore, old shipwrecks may be revealed. Fish may be stranded on the beach. People are often killed because they rush to pick up the fish. There may be a hissing and cracking sound, or a rumble like thunder, as the tsunami approaches.

▼ *The ocean receding from the coast of Kalutara, Sri Lanka, during the tsunami that struck in December 2004.*

Flooding

A tsunami is rarely a big breaking wave. Instead, the sea level swells and rises, and a flood washes in over the land. Froth and breaking waves come from the flood hitting features of the landscape and buildings, and from water falling over walls and through windows.

The behaviour of the wave depends very much on the shape and geographical features of the coastline. If there are lots of areas of coastline exposed, with inlets and promontories, a complex pattern of flooding can occur, with water coming in several directions. Sometimes a river can funnel a wave far inland, or a harbour can trap a wave so that it bounces backwards and forwards off the harbour walls.

Wave after wave

Tsunamis are really a 'wave train' with more waves following the first at an interval of anything from five to ninety minutes. People sometimes return to the area after the first wave, thinking the tsunami is over. They may then be killed or swept away by the next wave, which is frequently bigger than the first.

▲ *The tsunami flooding over Koh Racha Island, south of Phuket, Thailand, in December 2004.*

CRASHING WAVE

Very occasionally a tsunami can arrive as a giant breaking wave, called a bore. This is a vertical wave with a churning front and is extremely destructive because of the force with which it pounds the land. It may happen if the tsunami comes from deep water into a shallow bay or river.

Human Catastrophe

▼ *Survivors of the tsunami in 2004 view the wreckage of their home in Nagapattinam, India.*

A tsunami can wreak terrible devastation if it strikes a populated area. In some of the areas in the Pacific that are frequently hit by tsunamis, many people live by fishing and spend their whole lives on the shore, in the danger area. Tourist areas are also clustered along the coastlines.

Death and destruction

Drowning is not the only risk a tsunami brings. People may be thrown against hard objects by the force of the water, crushed by falling buildings, or hit by debris carried on the flood. They may be dragged out to sea as the tsunami recedes. Survivors can suffer terrible consequences if their homes and livelihoods are wrecked and their communities destroyed.

When the waters drop, the danger is far from over. Many of the countries where tsunamis occur are tropical or semi-tropical. Disease spreads quickly in hot, wet conditions. With no sanitation or clean water, and often with the dead bodies of people and animals lying unburied on land and in the water, cholera, diphtheria, typhoid, dysentery and other deadly diseases quickly take hold and spread. Disease can kill as many people as the tsunami itself.

Cut off

Often, roads, harbours and runways are swept away or rendered useless by flooding. They may be filled with debris or the surfaces destroyed. This makes it very difficult for aid to reach the stricken area and for injured people to be taken to safety. There may be no drinking water, food, emergency shelter or medical supplies for several days, especially in remote areas.

CASE STUDY

Indian Ocean, 2004

On 26 December 2004, an earthquake in the Indian Ocean off the northwest coast of the Indonesian island of Sumatra caused the most devastating tsunami in human history. The earthquake released as much energy as 23,000 atomic bombs. Nearly 300,000 people were killed or reported missing, most of them in Sumatra, Thailand, Sri Lanka and India, and more than a million people were made homeless. The area was left with destroyed communities and land that cannot be used, scattered with wreckage and stripped of vegetation. Waves from the tsunami were detected as far away as Antarctica and the coast of South America.

▲ *A village near the coast of Sumatra, Indonesia, lies in ruins after being destroyed by the 2004 tsunami.*

Helping Out

People struck by a tsunami need help immediately, and for months or years afterwards. After the emergency services have rescued people who are trapped, injured, or drifting in the sea, the next job is to provide food, shelter, water and medical help. And after that, the work of rebuilding lives and communities must begin.

▼ An injured tsunami victim is helped to a U.S. Navy helicopter in Banda Aceh, Indonesia, to be taken to hospital.

Emergency services

Police, coastguards, ambulance and fire services may all be involved in emergency relief. They are needed to rescue people from the water, from trees and rooftops where they have taken refuge, and from under debris and inside collapsed buildings. They must also take on the grim task of removing dead bodies.

If the tsunami is large and affects a wide area, local services may not be able to cope, or may be put out of action themselves. International aid can step in, with expert emergency teams, assistance from armed forces and charity or aid workers. If some areas are cut off by water, or by piles of debris, clearing routes to and within the disaster area is a crucial early stage of relief work.

Many ordinary people in the area may join the rescue efforts. Even without expert knowledge, they can give crucial help in locating people and helping them to safety.

Keeping in touch

If local communication links are destroyed, radio, mobile phones and computers with wireless Internet links are a crucial means of keeping in touch. In the Indian Ocean tsunami of 2004, survivors, volunteer helpers and aid workers used text messages to guide rescuers to trapped victims. They used blogs – diaries kept on a website – to keep the outside world updated.

▲ *Temporary homes on stilts house survivors of the tsunami in the Indian Ocean in 2004.*

CASE STUDY

Rescue, aid and rebuilding

Following the Indian Ocean tsunami of 26 December 2004, international emergency teams arrived quickly. The immediate aid needed in the area was water purification units, tents, medicines, food – especially baby food – and skilled medical staff. Money was donated by countries around the world, by individuals giving to charities and by international organizations such as the World Bank. A total of $7 billion was promised in the first month. The estimated cost of clearing up and rebuilding is more than $13 billion over several years.

Terrible Aftermath

The effects of a major tsunami can last years or even decades. For people who have lost family members, the effects last a lifetime. As well as the personal tragedies, the loss of communities, buildings, farmland and forest, and changes to the coast, often cause financial disaster, adding to the trauma for survivors.

Personal tragedies

A tsunami can kill large proportions of the local population, and many may lose a number of family members and friends. Often people are missing, with no body ever recovered, and many bodies that are recovered are not identifiable. Orphaned children, or those separated from their parents in the chaos, must be reunited with family members. With children too small or traumatized to communicate, this can be very difficult.

After the tsunami of 2004, photos taken with digital cameras and mobile phones were posted on the web or made into wall displays in local hospitals. These helped to identify lost survivors and bodies that had been recovered.

▶ *In Phuket, Thailand, survivors pick their way through the chaos after the 2004 tsunami.*

Broken communities

In some places, too few people are left alive to rebuild a community. In the Indian Ocean tsunami, many more women than men died, and local communities had to adapt to different social structures after the event.

A tsunami commonly destroys buildings, farms, fishing grounds, forest, roads and other amenities and natural areas that are vital to people living in the area. In the aftermath, many people cannot make a living and may have no home or shelter. The devastation can have a financial impact for many years. National and international aid is used to help people rebuild homes and establish a livelihood in the wrecked environment.

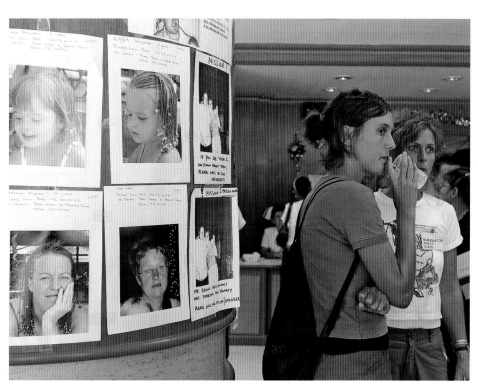

▲ *After the disaster, wall displays of photographs helped to identify people lost or killed during the tsunami in 2004.*

CASE STUDY

Papua New Guinea, 1998

On 17 July 1998, a ten-metre-high tsunami swept across a spit of land in Papua New Guinea with devastating results for the ten thousand inhabitants and their homes. The wave arrived without warning, following an earthquake only thirty kilometres away. Many of the victims were children, playing near the beaches during the school holiday. The community faces a difficult future with a whole generation lost. Raymond Nimis, a survivor, described what happened: 'I felt the earthquake rocking the house. It was dark. Then we heard the sea break. I saw it, very huge, we tried to run but it was too late.'

Environmental Impact

After a tsunami, the first concern is to help people. The impact on the environment is usually a secondary worry – but it can be closely bound up with the lives of local people, especially in areas where most live from fishing or farming.

▼ *Lituya Bay in Alaska, fourteen years after the largest tsunami ever recorded devastated the area in 1958.*

Devastation in the sea

The sea soon looks calm again after the tsunami has receded, but disastrous effects may be hidden beneath the surface. A tsunami can smash coral reefs apart, destroying the local marine habitat. Displaced rocks and coral are a peril to fishermen who once knew the shape of the land under the sea.

Rafts of debris washed from the land often include the dead bodies of people and animals. They clog bays and harbours and float far out to sea. They may block the flow of rivers into the sea, and as they decay, they may pollute the water or poison marine life. Pollution from damaged industrial sites on the coast poses a further danger to fish and seabirds.

GROWING BACK

Nature is remarkably resilient, and plants and animals soon return to a devastated region. Although whole forests may be swept away by a tsunami, fast-growing trees start to reappear within a year or two and animals start to move back in. Under the sea, repair is slower. It may take centuries for coral reefs to grow back after a major tsunami. Sometimes, objects washed into the sea can aid regrowth: corals and fish may start to inhabit the debris as an artificial reef and it eventually becomes part of the rebuilt reef.

▼ *Trees were felled and forests destroyed near Ban Nam Khen village in Thailand in December 2004.*

Inland destruction

Damage on land is more obvious. A wide area may be littered with debris, forests may be flattened and farmland flooded. Not all harm is visible, though. Salt water or pollution flooding fields may make them unusable for farming for years. Soil is often eroded or washed away, making the land unusable by people or animals.

Making matters worse

Human activity has an impact on the environment, too. Where people have destroyed or damaged coral reefs and mangrove forests, they have removed a barrier that could have protected them from tsunamis. The impact of a tsunami in the area is likely to be greater as it can sweep inland unhampered by these natural defences.

Rebuilding

▼ *A man mends the roof of a building destroyed by the tsunami in 2004 in Nagapattinam, India.*

It can take a very long time for an area to recover from a big tsunami. National and international efforts are often needed to address all the different areas of rebuilding, from cleaning up the environment to putting up new buildings, resettling communities and providing emotional and psychological help for victims.

Back to normal

It's very important for the people affected by a disaster to return to some sort of normal life as quickly as possible. Providing schools and at least temporary homes is a priority once the immediate needs for food, water and medicines have been met.

In building houses, there can be a conflict between people's desire to rebuild traditional homes and the advice of engineers and other experts on building to avoid future tsunami damage, either by building in a different place or using different methods. It is a sensitive issue that needs careful handling.

It is not just houses and businesses that are destroyed by a tsunami. Public facilities such as schools and hospitals must be rebuilt, roads and harbours must be repaired, and vital supplies such as water, electricity and communications networks must all be restored before normal life can resume.

A financial view

The financial cost of recreating whole communities can be immense. It is not just a case of providing people with a new home; they must also be able to continue to support themselves. A fishing community must always live near the coast. A tourist area will always need buildings on the seafront. People can only fully recover when their traditional industries have been restored.

▲ *Two volunteers run a temporary school set up to help children in Sri Lanka after the 2004 tsunami destroyed their regular school.*

CASE STUDY

Philippines (Moro Gulf), 1976

A tsunami and earthquake centred on the Cotabato Trench in the Celebes Sea killed more than seven thousand people in the Philippines on 17 August 1976. Ninety per cent of the deaths were caused by the tsunami, which swept away the whole of Pagadian City while the population slept.

Pagadian has been rebuilt and now has a population of 73,000. Most of the houses along the coast in Pagadian are made of wood, often supported on stilts. They were quick to rebuild, but are vulnerable to further tsunamis.

Keeping an Eye on Things

▼ *Since the tsunami of 1998, people living near the coast of Papua New Guinea have been encouraged to adopt a tree to climb if another tsunami hits. They can cut toe-holds in the trunk and know they have somewhere safe to go if necessary.*

Because tsunamis are caused by other events, they can't be predicted independently. Early warning systems either spot events which may trigger a tsunami, or identify a tsunami when it is on its way – there may then be little time left for people to escape.

Tsunami warning

Local early warning systems detect signs of earthquakes and the Earth's plates shifting to predict a possible tsunami. People are warned using sirens and public address systems. There are many false alarms, as it is not possible to tell whether a tsunami will actually occur.

Remote warning systems are more accurate and never give a false alarm. They use wave gauges and sea-floor pressure gauges to spot a sudden rise in sea level or rise in pressure on the seabed that means a tsunami has already started. The tsunami can then be modelled by a computer, and accurate predictions and warnings issued.

Watching from space

The tsunami in the Indian Ocean in 2004 was the first to be spotted by a satellite. Although the satellite registered a sixty-centimetre rise in sea level, it was not useful for warning people. It took five hours to process the information and it was only by chance that the satellite was passing the area at the appropriate time.

More usefully, satellites monitor the movement of tectonic plates and any telltale bulging of volcanoes, and so are able to give early warnings of eruptions or earthquakes that may trigger a tsunami.

Up against the wall

In some places, such as Japan and the Maldives, strong sea walls have been built in the hope of holding back a tsunami. But some experts believe a strong tsunami may smash down the walls, or simply sweep over the top. The second possibility is more dangerous, as people could then be crushed against the wall in the backwash.

◀ *Testing a new system that uses text messages to warn people about a tsunami approaching the area.*

AN EARLY WARNING SYSTEM FOR THE INDIAN OCEAN

After the disastrous Indian Ocean tsunami in 2004, work on an early warning system for the Indian Ocean has become a priority. A system of sea-floor pressure sensors will provide immediate warning of a tsunami. When pressure on the seabed increases because of a tsunami above it, a message will be sent by sonar to a buoy above the sensor. This will then send a radio warning to a tsunami warning centre by satellite, which will communicate with local coordinators by phone, radio, fax and email.

Where Next?

A tsunami can strike almost any area of coast. They most often start in areas where earthquakes and volcanic eruptions are likely, but can cross oceans to hit land. Freak events can even trigger tsunamis in areas where we might least expect them.

▲ *Were the dinosaurs wiped out by a meteorite? A large meteorite hitting the sea would start a monster tsunami.*

Looking ahead

Scientists try to identify places that may be in danger of a large tsunami because earthquakes or volcanic eruptions are likely either in the local area or across the sea. More quakes are likely in the Indian Ocean, for example, so Indonesia is still in danger.

Where volcanic eruptions have caused tsunamis in the past, they may well do so again. The Mediterranean could be in danger from an eruption of Mount Vesuvius in Italy, or a Greek island volcano. Japan is in danger of tsunamis both from local earthquakes and from quakes across the Pacific. Hawaii is in danger of tsunamis from earthquakes on the fault lines running around the west coast of the USA and Canada.

From outer space

In the past, some mega-tsunamis have been caused by meteorites landing in the sea. Geological evidence suggests that large tsunamis hitting the coast of Australia and New Zealand a few hundred years ago may have been caused by meteorites.

Scientists predict there is a one in three hundred chance of a huge meteorite, known as 1950 DA, hitting the Earth on 16 March 2880. It could cause a tsunami 120 metres high. Asteroids the size of 1950 DA have probably struck the Earth about six hundred times since the age of the dinosaurs – about once every 100,000 years.

MEGA-TSUNAMIS

A mega-tsunami is a giant tsunami, larger than any that humans have ever recorded. The last known mega-tsunami was four thousand years ago at Réunion Island in the Indian Ocean. The largest recorded wave was in Alaska in 1958, caused by a landslide. It was half a kilometre high.

Scientists think that when the volcano Cumbre Vieja in the Canary Islands erupts, a huge landslide may send five hundred thousand million tonnes of rock crashing into the Atlantic. A gigantic wave would race across the ocean and sweep away everything within twenty kilometres of the coast in North America and the Caribbean.

▼ *A tsunami from the Canary Islands could sweep across the Atlantic and destroy New York.*

KILLER TSUNAMIS

When	Where	Why	Casualties
c. 1410 BCE	Santorini (Thera), Greece	Volcanic eruption	c. 100,000 dead
20 September 1498	Nankaido, Japan	Earthquake	31,200 dead
28 October 1707	Tokaido-Nankaido, Japan	Earthquake	30,000 dead
22 May 1782	South China Sea	Earthquake	40,000 dead
13 August 1868	Northern Chile	Earthquake	25,674 dead
27 August 1883	Krakatau, Indonesia	Volcanic eruption	36,500 dead
15 June 1896	San Riku, Japan	Earthquake	26,360 dead
26 December 2004	Indian Ocean	Earthquake	c. 290,000 dead

GLOSSARY

backwash The movement of water draining back to the sea after a wave has broken.

blog A public diary or discussion kept on a web page.

bore A tsunami that arrives as a crashing, breaking wave.

cholera A disease carried in unclean water, causing sickness and diarrhoea.

crust The hard, outer layer of the Earth.

debris Wreckage.

diphtheria A disease that causes exhaustion, fever and difficulty in breathing and swallowing.

dysentery A disease carried in unclean water, causing severe diarrhoea.

earthquake A sudden, violent shaking of the land caused by the movement of tectonic plates.

epicentre The point on the Earth's surface that is directly above the place where an earthquake occurs.

erode Wear away.

eruption The ejection of hot, semi-liquid rock, gas and/or ash by a volcano.

friction Resistance produced by two surfaces rubbing together as one tries to move over the other.

geographical Relating to the features of the landscape.

geological Relating to rocks and minerals.

landslide A slippage of a large mass of rock or earth.

magma chamber The area beneath a volcano in which magma (molten rock) collects.

mangrove A tree that grows in flooded or very swampy land.

mantle A layer of the Earth formed of semi-liquid, moving, molten rock.

meteorite A lump of rock, ice or metal from space.

Minoan Relating to the Bronze Age culture of Crete that existed between 3000 and 1100 BCE.

promontory A piece of land that juts into the sea.

Richter scale A scale for measuring the intensity of earthquakes.

sonar Sound waves.

tectonic plates Vast slabs of the Earth's crust that carry oceans and continents.

typhoid A disease carried by unclean water, causing fever, a rash and abdominal pain.

volcano A hill or mountain where molten rock spurts to the surface from deep underground.

FURTHER INFORMATION

Books

Horrible Geography: Cracking Coasts by Anita Ganeri (Scholastic, 2006)

Tsunami! Death Wave (Cover-To-Cover Books) by Margo Sorenson (Perfection Learning, 1997)

Tsunami: Hope, Heroes and Incredible Stories of Survival by Joe Funk (editor), (Triumph Books, 2005)

Tsunami Man: Learning About Killer Waves with Walter Dudley by Anthony D. Fredericks (University of Hawaii Press, 2002)

Tsunami: Monster Waves (American Disasters) by Mary Dodson Wade and Janet Hamilton (Enslow, 2002)

Tsunami!: The 1946 Hilo Wave Of Terror (X-Treme Disasters That Changed America) by Scott Ingram (Bearport Publishing, 2005)

Tsunami: The World's Most Terrifying Natural Disaster by Geoff Tibballs (Carlton Books, 2005)

Websites

www.nationalgeographic.com/ngkids/9610/kwave/

www.bbc.co.uk/science/hottopics/naturaldisasters/tidalwaves.shtml

www.bbc.co.uk/science/horizon/2000/mega_tsunami.shtml

Videos/DVDs

The Day After Tomorrow directed by Robert Emmerich (Fox Home Entertainment, 2004)

Krakatoa, East of Java directed by Bernard L. Kowalski (MGM, 1969)

National Geographic: Tsunami – Killer Wave (Warner Home Video, 2005)

INDEX

Page numbers in **bold** refer to illustrations.